Therapy Notes for Families
Staying organized with your child's needs

A planner to keep you on track

Jenn T. Grace & Andrea Grace

Therapy Notes for Families
Staying organized with your child's needs

A planner to keep you on track

Jenn T. Grace
&
Andrea Grace

Copyright © 2016 Publish Your Purpose Press

All rights reserved.

No part of this publication shall be reproduced, transmitted, or sold in whole or in part in any form without prior written consent of the author. All trademarks and registered trademarks appearing in this guide are the property of their respective owners.

Published by Publish Your Purpose Press
141 Weston Street, #155, Hartford, CT 06141
www.PublishYourPurposePress.com

Written and created by:
Jenn T. Grace
Andrea Grace

Designed by:
Fi2 Design

ISBN-13: 978-1946384003
ISBN-10: 1946384003

First edition, December 2016.

Printed in the United States of America.

Dedicated to the strongest person I know: you.

Keep your head up - you've got this!

Background Information

The following pages are intended for you to keep track of all pertinent contact information related to your child's needs.

This may include clinicians;
Pediatrician
Psychiatrist
Neuropsychologist
Therapist

And school staff such as;
Principal
Psychologist
Social Worker
Classroom Teacher
Special Ed Teacher
School Nurse

Additional pages are located in the back

Background information

Name: _____
Date of Birth: _____
Birth Weight: _____
Birth Length: _____
Known Complications w/ Pregnancy: ____
_____
_____
_____
_____
_____

Milestones (age achieved)

Crawling: _____
Walking: _____
First Words: _____
First Sentences: _____
Other: _____

Education History (if so, when)

Retained in School: _____
IEP: _____
504: _____
Other: _____

Misc. Notes

Doctor and provider info

Name: _____
Title: _____
Address: _____
Phone Number: _____
Email Address: _____
Notes: _____
_____

Name: _____
Title: _____
Address: _____
Phone Number: _____
Email Address: _____
Notes: _____
_____

Name: _____
Title: _____
Address: _____
Phone Number: _____
Email Address: _____
Notes: _____
_____

Doctor and provider info

Name: _____
Title: _____
Address: _____
Phone Number: _____
Email Address: _____
Notes: _____
_____

Name: _____
Title: _____
Address: _____
Phone Number: _____
Email Address: _____
Notes: _____
_____

Name: _____
Title: _____
Address: _____
Phone Number: _____
Email Address: _____
Notes: _____
_____

More space is available in the back

School Information

Name: _____
Address: _____
Phone Number: _____
Fax Number: _____

Individual Information

Name: _____
Title: _____
Phone Number: _____
Email Address: _____
Notes: _____
_____

Name: _____
Title: _____
Phone Number: _____
Email Address: _____
Notes: _____
_____

Individual Information

Name: _____

Title: _____

Phone Number: _____

Email Address: _____

Notes: _____

_____

Name: _____

Title: _____

Phone Number: _____

Email Address: _____

Notes: _____

_____

Name: _____

Title: _____

Phone Number: _____

Email Address: _____

Notes: _____

_____

More space is available in the back

Medication History

Name: _____ Dosage: _____
Usage Directions: _____
Purpose/To Treat: _____
Start Date: _____ End Date: _____
Outcome/Results: _____
_____
_____

Name: _____ Dosage: _____
Usage Directions: _____
Purpose/To Treat: _____
Start Date: _____ End Date: _____
Outcome/Results: _____
_____
_____

Name: _____ Dosage: _____
Usage Directions: _____
Purpose/To Treat: _____
Start Date: _____ End Date: _____
Outcome/Results: _____
_____
_____

Medication History

Name: _____ Dosage: _____
Usage Directions: _____
Purpose/To Treat: _____
Start Date: _____ End Date: _____
Outcome/Results: _____
_____
_____

Name: _____ Dosage: _____
Usage Directions: _____
Purpose/To Treat: _____
Start Date: _____ End Date: _____
Outcome/Results: _____
_____
_____

Name: _____ Dosage: _____
Usage Directions: _____
Purpose/To Treat: _____
Start Date: _____ End Date: _____
Outcome/Results: _____
_____
_____

How to use this book

Sun (Mon) Tue Wed Thu Fri Sat

Clinician name: **Amanda** Clinician title: **Therapist**
Location: **333 Main St.** Date: **1/9/19** Time: **9:30am**

Height: **54"**
Weight: **68 lbs**
Blood Pressure: **114/83**

Medication Name/Dosage:
Trileptal, 150mg, 2x daily
Saphris, 2.5mg, 1x night

Family Notes: Don't forget to tell Amanda what happened at school on Friday. We had a challenging weekend - long lasting tantrum on Saturday.

Ask what she thinks about how we should prepare for the upcoming meeting at the school.

It's hard to tell if the dosage change in the Saphris is having any kind of impact. We'll keep watching to see.

Next visit on: **Jan. 16, 2019**   (over)

Comments from the clinician: Amanda thinks we should try new strategies and add more structure to the weekend to see if it'll help stop the tantrums.

She's reviewing her notes of the last couple of months to see if there is anything helpful for our next PPT meeting.

When we see the psychiatrist next, we should find out more about the effects of Saphris - no new information.

To-do list:
#1 Figure out what to do on Saturdays to make it better

#2 Look up past notes for school meeting

#3 Pick up prescription

"Strength grows in the moments when you think you can't go on but you keep going anyway."
— Unknown

Sun   Mon   Tue   Wed   Thu   Fri   Sat

Clinician name: _____ Clinician title: _____
Location: _____ Date: _____ Time: _____

```
Height:
Weight:
Blood Pressure:
```

```
Medication Name/Dosage:
```

Family Notes: _____
_____
_____
_____
_____
_____
_____
_____
_____
_____
_____
_____

Next visit on: _____ (over)

Comments from the clinician: _____

_____
_____
_____
_____
_____
_____
_____
_____
_____
_____
_____
_____
_____

To-do list:
#1 _____
_____
#2 _____
_____
#3 _____
_____

Sun   Mon   Tue   Wed   Thu   Fri   Sat

Clinician name: _____ Clinician title: _____
Location: _____ Date: _____ Time: _____

Height:

Weight:

Blood Pressure:

Medication Name/Dosage:

Family Notes: _____
_____
_____
_____
_____
_____
_____
_____
_____
_____
_____
_____

Next visit on: _____ (over)

Comments from the clinician: _____
_____
_____
_____
_____
_____
_____
_____
_____
_____
_____
_____
_____

To-do list:
#1 _____
_____
#2 _____
_____
#3 _____
_____

Sun   Mon   Tue   Wed   Thu   Fri   Sat

Clinician name: _____ Clinician title: _____
Location: _____ Date: _____ Time: _____

Height:

Weight:

Blood Pressure:

Medication Name/Dosage:

Family Notes: _____
_____
_____
_____
_____
_____
_____
_____
_____
_____
_____
_____

Next visit on: _____ (over)

Comments from the clinician: _____

_____
_____
_____
_____
_____
_____
_____
_____
_____
_____
_____
_____
_____
_____

To-do list:
#1 _____
_____
#2 _____
_____
#3 _____
_____

Sun   Mon   Tue   Wed   Thu   Fri   Sat

Clinician name: _____ Clinician title: _____
Location: _____ Date: _____ Time: _____

Height:

Weight:

Blood Pressure:

Medication Name/Dosage:

Family Notes: _____

_____
_____
_____
_____
_____
_____
_____
_____
_____
_____
_____
_____

Next visit on: _____ (over)

Comments from the clinician: _____

_____
_____
_____
_____
_____
_____
_____
_____
_____
_____
_____
_____

To-do list:
#1 _____
_____
#2 _____
_____
#3 _____
_____

Sun   Mon   Tue   Wed   Thu   Fri   Sat

Clinician name: _____ Clinician title: _____
Location: _____ Date: _____ Time: _____

Height:

Weight:

Blood Pressure:

Medication Name/Dosage:

Family Notes: _____
_____
_____
_____
_____
_____
_____
_____
_____
_____
_____
_____

Next visit on: _____   (over)

Comments from the clinician: _____

_____
_____
_____
_____
_____
_____
_____
_____
_____
_____
_____
_____

To-do list:
#1 _____
_____
#2 _____
_____
#3 _____
_____

Sun   Mon   Tue   Wed   Thu   Fri   Sat

Clinician name: _____ Clinician title: _____
Location: _____ Date: _____ Time: _____

Height:
Weight:
Blood Pressure:

Medication Name/Dosage:

Family Notes: _____
_____
_____
_____
_____
_____
_____
_____
_____
_____
_____
_____

Next visit on: _____ (over)

Comments from the clinician: _____
_____
_____
_____
_____
_____
_____
_____
_____
_____
_____
_____
_____
_____

To-do list:
#1 _____
_____
#2 _____
_____
#3 _____
_____

Sun   Mon   Tue   Wed   Thu   Fri   Sat

Clinician name: _____ Clinician title: _____
Location: _____ Date: _____ Time: _____

Height:

Weight:

Blood Pressure:

Medication Name/Dosage:

Family Notes: _____
_____
_____
_____
_____
_____
_____
_____
_____
_____
_____
_____

Next visit on: _____ (over)

Comments from the clinician: _____

To-do list:
#1 _____
#2 _____
#3 _____

Sun   Mon   Tue   Wed   Thu   Fri   Sat

Clinician name: _____ Clinician title: _____
Location: _____ Date: _____ Time: _____

Height:

Weight:

Blood Pressure:

Medication Name/Dosage:

Family Notes: _____
_____
_____
_____
_____
_____
_____
_____
_____
_____
_____
_____
_____

Next visit on: _____ (over)

Comments from the clinician: _____

_____
_____
_____
_____
_____
_____
_____
_____
_____
_____
_____
_____

To-do list:
#1 _____
_____
#2 _____
_____
#3 _____
_____

Sun   Mon   Tue   Wed   Thu   Fri   Sat

Clinician name: _____ Clinician title: _____
Location: _____ Date: _____ Time: _____

Height:

Weight:

Blood Pressure:

Medication Name/Dosage:

Family Notes: _____

_____
_____
_____
_____
_____
_____
_____
_____
_____
_____
_____

Next visit on: _____ (over)

Comments from the clinician: _____

_____
_____
_____
_____
_____
_____
_____
_____
_____
_____
_____
_____

To-do list:
#1 _____
_____
#2 _____
_____
#3 _____
_____

Sun   Mon   Tue   Wed   Thu   Fri   Sat

Clinician name: _____   Clinician title: _____
Location: _____ Date: _____ Time: _____

Height:

Weight:

Blood Pressure:

Medication Name/Dosage:

Family Notes: _____
_____
_____
_____
_____
_____
_____
_____
_____
_____
_____
_____

Next visit on: _____   (over)

Comments from the clinician: _____
_____
_____
_____
_____
_____
_____
_____
_____
_____
_____
_____
_____
_____
_____

To-do list:
#1 _____
_____
#2 _____
_____
#3 _____
_____

Sun   Mon   Tue   Wed   Thu   Fri   Sat

Clinician name: _____ Clinician title: _____
Location: _____ Date: _____ Time: _____

Height:

Weight:

Blood Pressure:

Medication Name/Dosage:

Family Notes: _____
_____
_____
_____
_____
_____
_____
_____
_____
_____
_____
_____
_____

Next visit on: _____ (over)

Comments from the clinician: _____

To-do list:
#1 _____
_____
#2 _____
_____
#3 _____
_____

Sun   Mon   Tue   Wed   Thu   Fri   Sat

Clinician name: _____ Clinician title: _____
Location: _____ Date: _____ Time: _____

Height:

Weight:

Blood Pressure:

Medication Name/Dosage:

Family Notes: _____
_____
_____
_____
_____
_____
_____
_____
_____
_____
_____
_____

Next visit on: _____ (over)

Comments from the clinician: _____

_____
_____
_____
_____
_____
_____
_____
_____
_____
_____
_____
_____
_____

To-do list:
#1 _____
_____
#2 _____
_____
#3 _____
_____

Sun   Mon   Tue   Wed   Thu   Fri   Sat

Clinician name: _____ Clinician title: _____
Location: _____ Date: _____ Time: _____

Height:

Weight:

Blood Pressure:

Medication Name/Dosage:

Family Notes: _____

_____
_____
_____
_____
_____
_____
_____
_____
_____
_____
_____

Next visit on: _____   (over)

Comments from the clinician: _____
_____
_____
_____
_____
_____
_____
_____
_____
_____
_____
_____
_____

To-do list:
#1 _____
_____
#2 _____
_____
#3 _____
_____

Sun   Mon   Tue   Wed   Thu   Fri   Sat

Clinician name: _____ Clinician title: _____
Location: _____ Date: _____ Time: _____

Height:

Weight:

Blood Pressure:

Medication Name/Dosage:

Family Notes: _____

_____
_____
_____
_____
_____
_____
_____
_____
_____
_____
_____

Next visit on: _____ (over)

Comments from the clinician: _____

_____
_____
_____
_____
_____
_____
_____
_____
_____
_____
_____

To-do list:
#1 _____
_____
#2 _____
_____
#3 _____
_____

Sun   Mon   Tue   Wed   Thu   Fri   Sat

Clinician name: _____   Clinician title: _____
Location: _____ Date: _____ Time: _____

Height:

Weight:

Blood Pressure:

Medication Name/Dosage:

Family Notes: _____
_____
_____
_____
_____
_____
_____
_____
_____
_____
_____
_____
_____

Next visit on: _____   (over)

Comments from the clinician: _____

_____
_____
_____
_____
_____
_____
_____
_____
_____
_____
_____
_____
_____

To-do list:
#1 _____
_____
#2 _____
_____
#3 _____
_____

Sun　　Mon　　Tue　　Wed　　Thu　　Fri　　Sat

Clinician name: _____ Clinician title: _____
Location: _____ Date: _____ Time: _____

Height:

Weight:

Blood Pressure:

Medication Name/Dosage:

Family Notes: _____
_____
_____
_____
_____
_____
_____
_____
_____
_____
_____
_____

Next visit on: _____ (over)

Comments from the clinician: _____
_____
_____
_____
_____
_____
_____
_____
_____
_____
_____
_____
_____

To-do list:
#1 _____
_____
#2 _____
_____
#3 _____
_____

Sun   Mon   Tue   Wed   Thu   Fri   Sat

Clinician name: _____   Clinician title: _____
Location: _____ Date: _____ Time: _____

Height:

Weight:

Blood Pressure:

Medication Name/Dosage:

Family Notes: _____
_____
_____
_____
_____
_____
_____
_____
_____
_____
_____
_____
_____

Next visit on: _____   (over)

Comments from the clinician: _____
_____
_____
_____
_____
_____
_____
_____
_____
_____
_____
_____
_____

To-do list:
#1 _____
_____
#2 _____
_____
#3 _____
_____

Sun   Mon   Tue   Wed   Thu   Fri   Sat

Clinician name: _____ Clinician title: _____
Location: _____ Date: _____ Time: _____

Height:

Weight:

Blood Pressure:

Medication Name/Dosage:

Family Notes: _____
_____
_____
_____
_____
_____
_____
_____
_____
_____
_____
_____

Next visit on: _____ (over)

Comments from the clinician: _____
_____
_____
_____
_____
_____
_____
_____
_____
_____
_____
_____
_____
_____

To-do list:
#1 _____
_____
#2 _____
_____
#3 _____
_____

Sun   Mon   Tue   Wed   Thu   Fri   Sat

Clinician name: _____   Clinician title: _____
Location: _____ Date: _____ Time: _____

```
Height:
Weight:
Blood Pressure:
```

```
Medication Name/Dosage:
```

Family Notes: _____
_____
_____
_____
_____
_____
_____
_____
_____
_____
_____
_____

Next visit on: _____   (over)

Comments from the clinician: _____

_____
_____
_____
_____
_____
_____
_____
_____
_____
_____
_____
_____
_____

To-do list:
#1 _____
_____
#2 _____
_____
#3 _____
_____

Sun   Mon   Tue   Wed   Thu   Fri   Sat

Clinician name: _____ Clinician title: _____
Location: _____ Date: _____ Time: _____

Height:

Weight:

Blood Pressure:

Medication Name/Dosage:

Family Notes: _____
_____
_____
_____
_____
_____
_____
_____
_____
_____
_____
_____

Next visit on: _____   (over)

Comments from the clinician: _____

_____
_____
_____
_____
_____
_____
_____
_____
_____
_____
_____
_____

To-do list:
#1 _____

#2 _____

#3 _____

Sun Mon Tue Wed Thu Fri Sat

Clinician name: _____ Clinician title: _____
Location: _____ Date: _____ Time: _____

Height:

Weight:

Blood Pressure:

Medication Name/Dosage:

Family Notes: _____

_____
_____
_____
_____
_____
_____
_____
_____
_____
_____
_____

Next visit on: _____ (over)

Comments from the clinician: _____
_____
_____
_____
_____
_____
_____
_____
_____
_____
_____
_____
_____
_____
_____

To-do list:
#1 _____
_____
#2 _____
_____
#3 _____
_____

Sun   Mon   Tue   Wed   Thu   Fri   Sat

Clinician name: _____   Clinician title: _____
Location: _____ Date: _____ Time: _____

```
Height:
Weight:
Blood Pressure:
```

```
Medication Name/Dosage:
```

Family Notes: _____
_____
_____
_____
_____
_____
_____
_____
_____
_____
_____

Next visit on: _____   (over)

Comments from the clinician: _____
_____
_____
_____
_____
_____
_____
_____
_____
_____
_____
_____
_____
_____

To-do list:
#1 _____
_____
#2 _____
_____
#3 _____
_____

Sun   Mon   Tue   Wed   Thu   Fri   Sat

Clinician name: _____ Clinician title: _____
Location: _____ Date: _____ Time: _____

Height:
Weight:
Blood Pressure:

Medication Name/Dosage:

Family Notes: _____
_____
_____
_____
_____
_____
_____
_____
_____
_____
_____
_____

Next visit on: _____ (over)

Comments from the clinician: _____

_____
_____
_____
_____
_____
_____
_____
_____
_____
_____
_____
_____

To-do list:
#1 _____
_____
#2 _____
_____
#3 _____
_____

Sun   Mon   Tue   Wed   Thu   Fri   Sat

Clinician name: _____ Clinician title: _____
Location: _____ Date: _____ Time: _____

Height:

Weight:

Blood Pressure:

Medication Name/Dosage:

Family Notes: _____

_____
_____
_____
_____
_____
_____
_____
_____
_____
_____
_____

Next visit on: _____ (over)

Comments from the clinician: _____

_____
_____
_____
_____
_____
_____
_____
_____
_____
_____
_____
_____

To-do list:
#1 _____
_____
#2 _____
_____
#3 _____
_____

Sun   Mon   Tue   Wed   Thu   Fri   Sat

Clinician name: _____ Clinician title: _____
Location: _____ Date: _____ Time: _____

Height:

Weight:

Blood Pressure:

Medication Name/Dosage:

Family Notes: _____
_____
_____
_____
_____
_____
_____
_____
_____
_____
_____
_____

Next visit on: _____ (over)

Comments from the clinician: _____
_____
_____
_____
_____
_____
_____
_____
_____
_____
_____
_____
_____
_____

To-do list:
#1 _____
_____
#2 _____
_____
#3 _____
_____

Sun   Mon   Tue   Wed   Thu   Fri   Sat

Clinician name: _____ Clinician title: _____
Location: _____ Date: _____ Time: _____

```
Height:
Weight:
Blood Pressure:
```

```
Medication Name/Dosage:
```

Family Notes: _____
_____
_____
_____
_____
_____
_____
_____
_____
_____
_____
_____

Next visit on: _____   (over)

Comments from the clinician: _____

_____
_____
_____
_____
_____
_____
_____
_____
_____
_____
_____

To-do list:
#1 _____
_____
#2 _____
_____
#3 _____
_____

Sun   Mon   Tue   Wed   Thu   Fri   Sat

Clinician name: _____ Clinician title: _____
Location: _____ Date: _____ Time: _____

Height:

Weight:

Blood Pressure:

Medication Name/Dosage:

Family Notes: _____
_____
_____
_____
_____
_____
_____
_____
_____
_____
_____
_____

Next visit on: _____ (over)

Comments from the clinician: _____
_____
_____
_____
_____
_____
_____
_____
_____
_____
_____
_____
_____
_____
_____

To-do list:
#1 _____
_____
#2 _____
_____
#3 _____
_____

Sun   Mon   Tue   Wed   Thu   Fri   Sat

Clinician name: _____ Clinician title: _____
Location: _____ Date: _____ Time: _____

Height:

Weight:

Blood Pressure:

Medication Name/Dosage:

Family Notes: _____
_____
_____
_____
_____
_____
_____
_____
_____
_____
_____
_____

Next visit on: _____ (over)

Comments from the clinician: _____
_____
_____
_____
_____
_____
_____
_____
_____
_____
_____
_____
_____
_____

To-do list:
#1 _____
_____
#2 _____
_____
#3 _____
_____

Sun   Mon   Tue   Wed   Thu   Fri   Sat

Clinician name: _____ Clinician title: _____
Location: _____ Date: _____ Time: _____

```
Height:
Weight:
Blood Pressure:
```

```
Medication Name/Dosage:
```

Family Notes: _____
_____
_____
_____
_____
_____
_____
_____
_____
_____
_____
_____
_____

Next visit on: _____ (over)

Comments from the clinician: _____

_____
_____
_____
_____
_____
_____
_____
_____
_____
_____
_____
_____

To-do list:
#1 _____
_____
#2 _____
_____
#3 _____
_____

Sun   Mon   Tue   Wed   Thu   Fri   Sat

Clinician name: _____ Clinician title: _____
Location: _____ Date: _____ Time: _____

Height:

Weight:

Blood Pressure:

Medication Name/Dosage:

Family Notes: _____
_____
_____
_____
_____
_____
_____
_____
_____
_____
_____
_____

Next visit on: _____ (over)

Comments from the clinician: _____

_____
_____
_____
_____
_____
_____
_____
_____
_____
_____
_____
_____
_____
_____

To-do list:
#1 _____
_____
#2 _____
_____
#3 _____
_____

Sun   Mon   Tue   Wed   Thu   Fri   Sat

Clinician name: _____ Clinician title: _____
Location: _____ Date: _____ Time: _____

Height:

Weight:

Blood Pressure:

Medication Name/Dosage:

Family Notes: _____
_____
_____
_____
_____
_____
_____
_____
_____
_____
_____
_____

Next visit on: _____ (over)

Comments from the clinician: _____

_____
_____
_____
_____
_____
_____
_____
_____
_____
_____
_____
_____
_____

To-do list:
#1 _____
_____

#2 _____
_____

#3 _____
_____

Sun   Mon   Tue   Wed   Thu   Fri   Sat

Clinician name: _____ Clinician title: _____
Location: _____ Date: _____ Time: _____

Height:

Weight:

Blood Pressure:

Medication Name/Dosage:

Family Notes: _____
_____
_____
_____
_____
_____
_____
_____
_____
_____
_____
_____
_____

Next visit on: _____ (over)

Comments from the clinician: _____

_____
_____
_____
_____
_____
_____
_____
_____
_____
_____
_____
_____
_____

To-do list:
#1 _____
_____
#2 _____
_____
#3 _____
_____

Sun Mon Tue Wed Thu Fri Sat

Clinician name: _____ Clinician title: _____
Location: _____ Date: _____ Time: _____

Height:

Weight:

Blood Pressure:

Medication Name/Dosage:

Family Notes: _____
_____
_____
_____
_____
_____
_____
_____
_____
_____
_____
_____

Next visit on: _____ (over)

Comments from the clinician: _____
_____
_____
_____
_____
_____
_____
_____
_____
_____
_____
_____
_____

To-do list:
#1 _____
_____
#2 _____
_____
#3 _____
_____

Sun   Mon   Tue   Wed   Thu   Fri   Sat

Clinician name: _____ Clinician title: _____
Location: _____ Date: _____ Time: _____

Height:

Weight:

Blood Pressure:

Medication Name/Dosage:

Family Notes: _____
_____
_____
_____
_____
_____
_____
_____
_____
_____
_____
_____

Next visit on: _____ (over)

Comments from the clinician: _____

_____
_____
_____
_____
_____
_____
_____
_____
_____
_____
_____
_____

To-do list:
#1 _____
_____
#2 _____
_____
#3 _____
_____

Sun   Mon   Tue   Wed   Thu   Fri   Sat

Clinician name: _____ Clinician title: _____
Location: _____ Date: _____ Time: _____

Height:

Weight:

Blood Pressure:

Medication Name/Dosage:

Family Notes: _____

_____
_____
_____
_____
_____
_____
_____
_____
_____
_____
_____
_____

Next visit on: _____ (over)

Comments from the clinician: _____

_____
_____
_____
_____
_____
_____
_____
_____
_____
_____
_____
_____
_____

To-do list:
#1 _____
_____
#2 _____
_____
#3 _____
_____

Sun   Mon   Tue   Wed   Thu   Fri   Sat

Clinician name: _____ Clinician title: _____
Location: _____ Date: _____ Time: _____

- Height:
- Weight:
- Blood Pressure:

Medication Name/Dosage:

Family Notes: _____
_____
_____
_____
_____
_____
_____
_____
_____
_____
_____
_____

Next visit on: _____ (over)

Comments from the clinician: _____

_____
_____
_____
_____
_____
_____
_____
_____
_____
_____
_____
_____

To-do list:
#1 _____
_____
#2 _____
_____
#3 _____
_____

Sun   Mon   Tue   Wed   Thu   Fri   Sat

Clinician name: _____ Clinician title: _____
Location: _____ Date: _____ Time: _____

Height:

Weight:

Blood Pressure:

Medication Name/Dosage:

Family Notes: _____
_____
_____
_____
_____
_____
_____
_____
_____
_____
_____
_____

Next visit on: _____ (over)

Comments from the clinician: _____

_____
_____
_____
_____
_____
_____
_____
_____
_____
_____
_____
_____

To-do list:
#1 _____
_____
#2 _____
_____
#3 _____
_____

Sun   Mon   Tue   Wed   Thu   Fri   Sat

Clinician name: _____ Clinician title: _____
Location: _____ Date: _____ Time: _____

Height:

Weight:

Blood Pressure:

Medication Name/Dosage:

Family Notes: _____
_____
_____
_____
_____
_____
_____
_____
_____
_____
_____
_____
_____

Next visit on: _____ (over)

Comments from the clinician: _____

_____
_____
_____
_____
_____
_____
_____
_____
_____
_____
_____
_____

To-do list:
#1 _____
_____
#2 _____
_____
#3 _____
_____

Sun   Mon   Tue   Wed   Thu   Fri   Sat

Clinician name: _____ Clinician title: _____
Location: _____ Date: _____ Time: _____

Height:

Weight:

Blood Pressure:

Medication Name/Dosage:

Family Notes: _____

_____

_____

_____

_____

_____

_____

_____

_____

_____

_____

_____

Next visit on: _____ (over)

Comments from the clinician: _____
_____
_____
_____
_____
_____
_____
_____
_____
_____
_____
_____
_____
_____

To-do list:
#1 _____
_____
#2 _____
_____
#3 _____
_____

Sun   Mon   Tue   Wed   Thu   Fri   Sat

Clinician name: _____ Clinician title: _____
Location: _____ Date: _____ Time: _____

```
Height:
Weight:
Blood Pressure:
```

```
Medication Name/Dosage:
```

Family Notes: _____
_____
_____
_____
_____
_____
_____
_____
_____
_____
_____
_____

Next visit on: _____   (over)

Comments from the clinician: _____

_____
_____
_____
_____
_____
_____
_____
_____
_____
_____
_____
_____
_____

To-do list:
#1 _____
_____
#2 _____
_____
#3 _____
_____

Sun   Mon   Tue   Wed   Thu   Fri   Sat

Clinician name: _____ Clinician title: _____
Location: _____ Date: _____ Time: _____

Height:

Weight:

Blood Pressure:

Medication Name/Dosage:

Family Notes: _____
_____
_____
_____
_____
_____
_____
_____
_____
_____
_____
_____
_____

Next visit on: _____ (over)

Comments from the clinician: _____

_____
_____
_____
_____
_____
_____
_____
_____
_____
_____
_____

To-do list:
#1 _____
_____
#2 _____
_____
#3 _____
_____

Sun   Mon   Tue   Wed   Thu   Fri   Sat

Clinician name: _____ Clinician title: _____
Location: _____ Date: _____ Time: _____

Height:

Weight:

Blood Pressure:

Medication Name/Dosage:

Family Notes: _____
_____
_____
_____
_____
_____
_____
_____
_____
_____
_____
_____

Next visit on: _____ (over)

Comments from the clinician: _____

_____
_____
_____
_____
_____
_____
_____
_____
_____
_____
_____
_____
_____
_____
_____

To-do list:
#1 _____
_____
#2 _____
_____
#3 _____
_____

Sun   Mon   Tue   Wed   Thu   Fri   Sat

Clinician name: _____ Clinician title: _____
Location: _____ Date: _____ Time: _____

Height:

Weight:

Blood Pressure:

Medication Name/Dosage:

Family Notes: _____
_____
_____
_____
_____
_____
_____
_____
_____
_____
_____

Next visit on: _____ (over)

Comments from the clinician: _____

_____
_____
_____
_____
_____
_____
_____
_____
_____
_____
_____
_____
_____

To-do list:
#1 _____
_____
#2 _____
_____
#3 _____
_____

Sun   Mon   Tue   Wed   Thu   Fri   Sat

Clinician name: _____ Clinician title: _____
Location: _____ Date: _____ Time: _____

Height:
Weight:
Blood Pressure:

Medication Name/Dosage:

Family Notes: _____
_____
_____
_____
_____
_____
_____
_____
_____
_____
_____
_____

Next visit on: _____ (over)

Comments from the clinician: _____
_____
_____
_____
_____
_____
_____
_____
_____
_____
_____
_____
_____

To-do list:
#1 _____
_____
#2 _____
_____
#3 _____
_____

Sun   Mon   Tue   Wed   Thu   Fri   Sat

Clinician name: _____   Clinician title: _____
Location: _____   Date: _____   Time: _____

Height:

Weight:

Blood Pressure:

Medication Name/Dosage:

Family Notes: _____
_____
_____
_____
_____
_____
_____
_____
_____
_____
_____
_____

Next visit on: _____   (over)

Comments from the clinician: _____

_____
_____
_____
_____
_____
_____
_____
_____
_____
_____
_____

To-do list:
#1 _____
_____
#2 _____
_____
#3 _____
_____

Sun   Mon   Tue   Wed   Thu   Fri   Sat

Clinician name: _____ Clinician title: _____
Location: _____ Date: _____ Time: _____

Height:

Weight:

Blood Pressure:

Medication Name/Dosage:

Family Notes: _____
_____
_____
_____
_____
_____
_____
_____
_____
_____
_____
_____

Next visit on: _____ (over)

Comments from the clinician: _____

_____
_____
_____
_____
_____
_____
_____
_____
_____
_____
_____
_____

To-do list:
#1 _____
_____
#2 _____
_____
#3 _____
_____

Sun   Mon   Tue   Wed   Thu   Fri   Sat

Clinician name: _____ Clinician title: _____
Location: _____ Date: _____ Time: _____

Height:

Weight:

Blood Pressure:

Medication Name/Dosage:

Family Notes: _____
_____
_____
_____
_____
_____
_____
_____
_____
_____
_____
_____
_____

Next visit on: _____ (over)

Comments from the clinician: _____

_____
_____
_____
_____
_____
_____
_____
_____
_____
_____
_____
_____

To-do list:
#1 _____
_____
#2 _____
_____
#3 _____
_____

Sun   Mon   Tue   Wed   Thu   Fri   Sat

Clinician name: _____ Clinician title: _____
Location: _____ Date: _____ Time: _____

Height:

Weight:

Blood Pressure:

Medication Name/Dosage:

Family Notes: _____

_____
_____
_____
_____
_____
_____
_____
_____
_____
_____
_____

Next visit on: _____ (over)

Comments from the clinician: _____
_____
_____
_____
_____
_____
_____
_____
_____
_____
_____
_____
_____
_____

To-do list:
#1 _____
_____
#2 _____
_____
#3 _____
_____

Sun   Mon   Tue   Wed   Thu   Fri   Sat

Clinician name: _____ Clinician title: _____
Location: _____ Date: _____ Time: _____

Height:

Weight:

Blood Pressure:

Medication Name/Dosage:

Family Notes: _____
_____
_____
_____
_____
_____
_____
_____
_____
_____
_____
_____

Next visit on: _____   (over)

Comments from the clinician: _____
_____
_____
_____
_____
_____
_____
_____
_____
_____
_____
_____
_____
_____
_____

To-do list:
#1 _____
_____
#2 _____
_____
#3 _____
_____

Sun　Mon　Tue　Wed　Thu　Fri　Sat

Clinician name: _____ Clinician title: _____
Location: _____ Date: _____ Time: _____

Height:

Weight:

Blood Pressure:

Medication Name/Dosage:

Family Notes: _____
_____
_____
_____
_____
_____
_____
_____
_____
_____
_____
_____

Next visit on: _____ (over)

Comments from the clinician: _____

_____
_____
_____
_____
_____
_____
_____
_____
_____
_____
_____
_____
_____

To-do list:
#1 _____
_____
#2 _____
_____
#3 _____
_____

Sun   Mon   Tue   Wed   Thu   Fri   Sat

Clinician name: _____ Clinician title: _____
Location: _____ Date: _____ Time: _____

Height:

Weight:

Blood Pressure:

Medication Name/Dosage:

Family Notes: _____
_____
_____
_____
_____
_____
_____
_____
_____
_____
_____
_____

Next visit on: _____   (over)

Comments from the clinician: _____

_____
_____
_____
_____
_____
_____
_____
_____
_____
_____
_____
_____
_____

To-do list:
#1 _____
_____
#2 _____
_____
#3 _____
_____

Sun   Mon   Tue   Wed   Thu   Fri   Sat

Clinician name: _____ Clinician title: _____
Location: _____ Date: _____ Time: _____

Height:

Weight:

Blood Pressure:

Medication Name/Dosage:

Family Notes: _____
_____
_____
_____
_____
_____
_____
_____
_____
_____
_____
_____

Next visit on: _____ (over)

Comments from the clinician: _____

_____
_____
_____
_____
_____
_____
_____
_____
_____
_____
_____
_____
_____

To-do list:
#1 _____
_____

#2 _____
_____

#3 _____
_____

Extra Contact Information

Name: _____
Title: _____
Address: _____
Phone Number: _____
Email Address: _____
Notes: _____
_____

Name: _____
Title: _____
Address: _____
Phone Number: _____
Email Address: _____
Notes: _____
_____

Name: _____
Title: _____
Address: _____
Phone Number: _____
Email Address: _____
Notes: _____
_____

Name: _____
Title: _____
Address: _____
Phone Number: _____
Email Address: _____
Notes: _____
_____

Name: _____
Title: _____
Address: _____
Phone Number: _____
Email Address: _____
Notes: _____
_____

Name: _____
Title: _____
Address: _____
Phone Number: _____
Email Address: _____
Notes: _____
_____

Misc. Notes

Attention Providers

If you would like multiple copies of this book for your patients or if you would like to put your name and/or logo on the front cover

please visit
www.TherapyNotesForFamilies.com
or email
TherapyNotesForFamilies@gmail.com

www.TherapyNotesForFamilies.com

www.ingramcontent.com/pod-product-compliance
Lightning Source LLC
Chambersburg PA
CBHW070945230426
43666CB00011B/2572